My Story

My Story copyright © 2015 by Gisele Baer.

Published through CreateSpace. First Edition.

ISBN-13: 978-0692391754
ISBN-10: 0692391754

Cover Design by Francis Bonnet
Marketing/Promotion by KLB Services
Edited by Karen Bonnet

My Story

By
Gisele
Baer

1

It's 1945, and I am 15 years-old. I think a lot about France, my native country, and all that has happened since we left.

Up until that fateful day in June 1940, we had a happy and carefree life. We lived in a large apartment in Paris, in a nice neighborhood. The summers were spent with my grandmother in the country, an hour by train from Paris. She lived in a small wooden house, with outdoor facilities. The beauty for us was the freedom to run outside and play all sorts of games with very little supervision. In the winters, she would live with us. That was to change soon.

Every day, we listened to the radio and heard the terrifying news threatening us. The Germans were getting closer! Many alarms sounded at night. When that happened, it became a habit to lay out clothes and shoes at the ready. Then, we would run down the stairs to the cellar. Jeannette, who was only three years-old, couldn't understand the whole ritual.

Dad was working as an accountant for a big organization called the Joint Distribution Committee (we referred to it as "The Joint"). They helped refugees from all over the world to relocate. For some reason he was called to Bordeaux to work, and we were going to join him later, but mom was getting very nervous listening to the bad news every day, so she decided, *"Enough!"* and started packing. Grandma was there, silently helping her.

We closed the door to our beautiful apartment, which had been completely renovated and newly furnished two years earlier. We went down the stairs, crossed the courtyard and stopped to say goodbye to our concierge. Out on the sidewalk, we hoped to catch a taxi. We walked, but none would stop. Soon we came to a corner and couldn't t help follow the delicious smell of bread. When the sales lady heard where we were headed, all she could say was she was sure we would never make it to the railroad station. First, it was impossible to get a taxi, and she had heard that there were thousands of people trying to flee.

We were out on the boulevard again. Of course, mom was not going to give up so quickly. All of a sudden, like magic, a taxi stopped in front of us, a lady stepped out, and we were in.

The chauffeur told us he had just come back from the railroad station. There was a mob of people; you could not get near it, and so he turned around. Determined, mom said, "we will try it," and so we were on our way. I was watching all the cafes and beautiful boulevards go by, not really concerned about when I would see them again. This was going to be temporary. We would wait it out until it was safe to return.

The taxi stopped suddenly; there was no railroad station in sight, only a mob of people and it was impossible to go further. We got off and just followed the crowd which was moving slowly and sometimes not at all. We spotted a bench, and quickly ran to it. Mom told Grandma to sit and wait with Jeanette and the luggage, so she could move faster and assess the situation.

Mom saw a policeman, the first one we could find, and showed him some papers which she hoped would ease her way to the train. But the policeman laughed at them and told her they were of no use. Discouraged, we started back to my grandmother, but just then, miraculously, the crowd was really moving. We rushed to her, and then joined in. Sometimes it moved and then it would stop completely. We put our suitcases down, and then resumed the march again. We were terrified to get separated. Jeannette held mother's skirt tightly, and Suzy and I kept very close to each other. Grandma was silent and never complained.

The policemen were screaming at us because mom was pushing her way in, and we had to follow her. This went on for hours; it was hard to ignore the crying of children who lost their parents, and old people fainting from the heat and fatigue. Then, with relief, we saw the building in the distance and soon came to a large grill door. The police were letting people through a few at a time. Mom bought our tickets and we sat down, exhausted, and had something to eat. It was 4:00 in the afternoon.

We waited for the train.

It came thundering down and sent an electric shock through us. We climbed aboard and chose our seats but grandma was still on the platform, holding Jeannette; she said she wanted to take some air, as it was very warm. All of a sudden, the train started moving and she quickly handed Jeannette to mom through the open window. I don t know if this was a last minute decision or she knew all along she was not leaving Paris. Her son was in the army and she wanted to be there when he came back, I think. I watched her, standing tall and straight, and when I could no longer see her, I cried uncontrollably. It was pretty much what you heard all around you.

Eventually, everybody settled themselves down and we started to enjoy the scenery. The countryside had a calming effect on us; those fields and small towns looked so peaceful. I woke up to screams of panic, "turn off the lights, turn off the lights". What was happening? Soon we knew. A bomb exploded near our train, illuminating our compartment. Jeannette was crying on mom's lap, and Suzy and I just sat paralyzed with fear. A few more distant explosions and it was over. People discussed the event for awhile, and then it was quiet again.

I woke up to sunshine gleaming on the waters of the Gironde. Bordeaux could not be too far. Each of us washed as best we could. It was 9:00 a.m. The landscape was pleasant to look at.

We pulled into the station, and it was bustling with people and luggage everywhere. We slowly made our way out on the sidewalk, and looked around for father. Mom, with her usual impatience, called a taxi and just as we stepped inside, dad appeared.

2

BORDEAUX

It was a little disconcerting to see him clean, well dressed, and full of pep. Everything we were not! He told us he had reserved two rooms at a hotel across the street. What a relief.

The first thing we did was to satisfy our appetite with a delicious meal. Then he took us to our room. All I saw was two beds, and in no time, we were fast asleep. When I woke up I was completely confused, not knowing which day it was or what hour for that matter. Suzy was just waking up too, but Jeannette was still sleeping soundly. Where were our parents? We couldn't leave Jeannette alone, so we waited for her to wake from slumber, then we all went downstairs to investigate.

A young woman came toward us, and I recognized her from the Paris office. "How was your trip?" she inquired. Just then our parents heard us and came to scoop us up, and everything was fine.

While all this was going on, Paris was being invaded. How narrowly we escaped! It wasn't long before Suzy and I found a new distraction—the elevator. We rode it constantly until it broke.

We spent a week in Bordeaux. Mom and Dad were worried. To be across from a railroad station was not exactly safe. Father's office building happened to have some empty rooms. That same evening, we moved and settled ourselves there, temporarily, of course. Mom and dad were in one room with Jeannette, while Suzy and I stayed in another.

Children that we were, we soon found a new diversion. Dad allowed us to use the different color stationary. Also, we had permission to type on the typewriter, and so we decided to write grandma a long letter about our adventures.

When night came, we did as we were trained to do in Paris. We laid our clothes at the ready in case of an alarm—and it came that night! We promptly dressed and went to mom and dad's room. To our surprise, they were in bed with no intentions of getting up. "Go back to bed," they said, "it's nothing." Just then the house shook with a nearby explosion. Mom grabbed Jeannette and ran out the door with nothing on but her nightgown. A woman was just passing her on the way down, and seeing her dressed like that, told her to go back and cover herself. Mom answered, "There is no time!" This same woman went in the room and grabbed the first thing she saw, and covered mom with it.

There were a lot of people in that cellar, but we were the only children. Nobody spoke, except an eccentric who kept going out to give us news. He said he saw German planes right over us; that's when he ran back in. Sure enough, we heard bombs explode all around us. I guess we felt pretty safe in that cellar because I don't remember being terribly scared. After awhile, the siren sounded and it was safe to return.

In the morning, we learned that the railroad station had been bombed and the hotel where we stayed had casualties. Two bombardments in one week was too much for mom's nerves, and she told dad that she was not staying another day. Somehow, it was arranged for a car to take us out of Bordeaux, but we could not take all our luggage with us. The Joint took charge of that, and we were on our way.

3

LA BOUHYERE

I can't remember how many hours we traveled. I don't know what arrangements mom and dad made with the driver. We were children, and as such we were not told anything. The car stopped right outside of town. We got out, and the driver left. Here we were, the five of us, standing on the sidewalk with our suitcases. After a while, it was decided that we children would wait with the luggage, and both mom and dad would walk around and hopefully find a place to stay.

We sat on our luggage and waited. I looked with worry at the sky that was getting dark, and Suzy made it worse by making fun of me. Big drops started to fall, so we ran for shelter under a tree. Luckily, our parents came back and we all checked into a small hotel. The next day, mom went to look for an apartment, but all she could find was one room in one house, and another room, five minutes away. We took it and Suzy and I stayed in the house that was five minutes away from our parents. We were delighted!

Each morning, after a good night sleep, we washed and went to join the rest of the family. We loved the morning walk and our independence. To get into our bed at night, Suzy had to push me from behind because it was so high. Once on the bed, I extended my arms to her and we were finally able to sleep.

The rains seemed to arrive with us, and all we could do was walk in the garden in our wooden shoes. Behind the row of houses were dense forests called "Les Landes." It seemed to me, the world ended there. Between those forests and the houses ran a brook. On nice days we would sit and soak our feet in it, singing our favorite songs. We were never bored. But this simple and peaceful life could not last forever.

One morning we woke up to disturbing news. A neighbor was telling everybody she met, that she had just returned from town and Germans in uniform were everywhere. Mom had to see for herself, and we went with her. Sure enough, there was hardly a street without seeing those horrible uniforms.

We walked into a store and a German was trying to tell a salesgirl in bad French that he wanted a knife. A chill went through me. A table knife, he finally explained. Okay, that calmed our fears somewhat!

We went home, mom determined to leave as soon as possible. She thought even a taxi would do, as long as we were out of here. She was not successful right away. Finally, one evening, she came home triumphant. She had met a woman, who like us, was looking to get out of town. Together, they came up with two milk trucks that were leaving for Agens. Money settled everything and we started packing.

We said our goodbyes to the kind people who housed us and we were ready to go.

Milk trucks only have seats in front, so this is how we worked out. In one truck were the driver, mom, dad and Jeannette. In the other, a second driver, Suzy, me, the lady, and her two dogs. Yes, it was pretty hot in July with those two dogs on your lap!

I don t remember feeling too emotional about this sudden departure. I watched the scenery. I guess I was too young and just took things pretty much in stride. My parents were not upset, so I wasn't t either. When I think of it today, I am filled with sadness.

The trip lasted all day. We stopped for lunch on the side of the road near a small lake. Mom took out a tablecloth and laid out all our provisions, including wine. We ate, drank to everybody s health, and packed up again.

We were riding awhile, when suddenly, out of nowhere, we saw soldiers blocking the road. The truck ahead of us stopped, and we were just behind them. A few soldiers approached. Dad showed them some papers; there was some discussion back and forth, and finally, they moved toward us. We were watching all this nervously, of course. I was so scared I was looking down the all time, not daring to meet their eyes, but, unexpectedly, I felt a hand caress my hair and the German said, Little children, dogs, I have home too." Then he smiled to the lady, waved his hand, and we were free to go and enter the "Free Zone."

It was late when we arrived in Agens. There was no place to sleep. Our driver was kind enough to give us his room for the night. There was only one bed but four of us were happy to share it. Dad, the lady, and two drivers slept in the trucks.

The next day, after breakfast, we said goodbye to our wonderful drivers and the cheerful lady, and each went his own way. That same afternoon we left on a truck with other refugees to Montignac Toupinerie in the Lot et Garonne region.

It was an uneventful trip. The sun had already gone down when we arrived. The Mayor of the town greeted us with these words," My friends, I regret to say there is nothing to eat here." As a response, women started to cry, Mom included, and asked why we were brought here. The Mayor tried to calm everybody down, and came to this solution: Every farm would take in one family. The one that was designated for us was not too large but the couple who owned it were elderly and very kind. We never ate better!

4

MONTIGNAC TOUPINERIE

How did we spend our time in this peaceful countryside? It was heaven for us; we were out all day either chasing the butterflies, or sitting on a bench knitting, right in front of the house. The elderly couple was charming and warm. Sometimes they took us to visit their neighbors in the evening. I loved our walks through the fields.

One morning, dad, Suzy, and I took some baskets and went apricot picking. We climbed up the tree and threw the apricots we picked in the basket. Of course, as many fell on the ground around that basket than in it. What wonderful fun it was. Mom got busy later making marmalade. It was impossible to stay away from those delicious fruits. Result: we were all sick next day.

Life was so sweet and simple here, we almost forgot we were at war. The Germans were advancing and we soon began to think of moving on.

Madame Boulain prepared a delicious dinner on our last day; then she walked with us as far as she could. We were crying and hugging her. We had become very attached to those good people. We arrived in town where a car took us to a railroad station called Marmandes.

5

CAVAILLON

We had a cleaning lady in Paris who came from Cavaillon, and she couldn't stop talking about her birthplace. What wonderful climate, how kind people were. It was decided to go there directly. The first few days, we stayed in a hotel, until mom found a two-room furnished apartment. It would do for the time being.

As soon as schools opened, we were registered and life returned to near normal. Even Jeannette started kindergarten. I took her on her first day but she wouldn't t let go of my skirt, so I had to stay with her. The second day, she wanted very much to play like the other children, so she let go of me and that s when I escaped. Outside the yard, I was able to watch her over a short wall. After that, it was easy. She loved school.

We all enjoyed this town. The air was balmy, the fruits plentiful and delicious. We moved into a larger apartment after a while, in a two-story building. The owner, a single lady , lived downstairs. Part was her living quarters, and part was a store, all lingerie and lace everywhere. We loved to visit and admire the merchandise. Madame Jaboulet was tall and stout with red hair, combed high. She smiled all the time, and was constantly moving. She loved to tell stories and had a captive audience with us.

Another attraction was her collection of spy books which she kept in the attic. Before long, we spent a lot of time there looking for something to read—of course, with the owner's permission.

Dad was working in Marseille and he would come and visit every weekend. The Joint didn't have an office in Cavaillon.

Winter came, cold and dry at first, and then one day we woke up to snow on all the red roofs of Cavaillon. Children of all ages were energized by this new diversion, and were throwing snow balls to anyone on their paths.

On Christmas Eve, Madame Jaboulet came up to see us and spent the evening delighting us with her many stories. Unfortunately, we had to leave and move to Marseille. It was the practical thing to do and economical too.

The day before our departure, our kind landlady invited us all to the movies. She had gotten attached to us and was sorry to see us go. We were sad too, because she was good company.

Gisele
and
Suzy

Pictured from left to right, Suzy, Jean, Rachel, Jeannette, Gisele.

My grandmother,
my mother,
Jeanette, Gisele
and Suzy

6

MARSEILLE

What a disappointment was that city; dirty and old-looking. During our whole stay, we were in a hotel. It was cold that winter and so was the hotel room. There were restrictions on bread, milk, and oil. Sometimes we would stand in line a long time, and there would be nothing left when it was our turn.

Again we started school, since we didn't t know how long we would remain in Marseille. Mom was sick with strep throat, her weakness, and Suzy had to stay home to care for her and Jeannette. These were very sad days in that cold hotel room.

One day Suzy picked me up in school and told me we had to go immediately to have pictures taken. That was when we first learned mom and dad were planning to go to America. We couldn't believe it!

After learning about our upcoming move, every time we received an important paper, we went to a nice restaurant to celebrate, and ate to our hearts content; something we couldn't do every day.

March came and our trip to America seemed more and more reality than a dream. On my last day of school, I promised my friends I would send them bananas, pineapples, and oranges once we were settled.

We had never been anywhere, and the notion of seeing another world, one that everybody dreamed about, was overwhelming. The thought of leaving my country did not make me sad. That would come much later.

On the 28th of March, we were ready. Mom was sad; but Suzy and I were so excited! We were going to a small island called the Dominican Republic. Nobody ever heard of it and nobody knew where it was, except of course, The Joint. They were instrumental in guiding us all the way, and deciding where to go. The idea crossed my mind that maybe it was very primitive, and we wouldn't t have to go to school. All you did all day long was climb trees and throw coconuts around. Also, we might be the only white people on the island! We took a map and tried to find where it was. I am not sure we found it...

We had become accustomed to leaving one place and settling somewhere else without any problem. Deep down, we always thought this was temporary, and we were just biding our time until the war ended. But now, we were leaving France. I was only 11, and did not at all comprehend the significance of this departure.

7

NEW HORIZONS

We were to take the train from Marseille, through Spain, to Lisbon, where our ship would take us to America, and for the first time in my life, I was watching in awe at the Pyrenees covered in snow. We arrived in Canfrant, ate, and took another train. That one was so packed, we could hardly move. I had to use the facilities, and didn't t know how I was going to make it. They carried me from one to the other to my destination. What an embarrassment!

We arrived in Madrid at 11:00 a.m. the next morning. A room had been reserved in advance for the day on a very well known Plaza, "La Puerta del Sol." The room was magnificent. I had never seen anything like it. We rested, then went to a nice restaurant to eat, and boarded the train to Lisbon that evening.

This part of the trip was a little more comfortable, as we were able to stretch out. The morning found us more rested. It was fun and interesting to watch the people when the train pulled into a station. The Spanish women were so dark and exotic looking.

After three days of travel, we arrived in Lisbon. It was 4:00 p.m. We were greeted by a gentleman from the Joint. He took us to a very nice hotel in the center of town. We had a large room with two beds; it was, in general, very comfortable and pleasant.

We had room service in the morning. I think I will always remember the small rolls. We ate like there was no tomorrow during the next few days.

While walking around the lobby, Suzy and I noticed two young girls about our age, reading a large book, which, when we got a little closer, happened to be in

French. The older girl noticed and came straight to us with a smile. And so started a wonderful friendship all the time we were in Lisbon. The two sisters were Dutch, on their way to Java. We became inseparable, playing hide-and-seek in the large and elegant lobby. We ran, we sang, we danced, and nobody ever stopped us. The whole hotel was ours. We often went for walks together. I forgot to mention that they spoke French fluently.

Suzy had her 13th birthday while still in Lisbon. For that occasion, we were treated with our friends to pastries in a cafe. Unfortunately, we all took our turn getting sick from overeating, and it was Suzy's turn that day.

For fun, we tried to imitate the Portuguese words we heard on the street. We spent 12 days in Lisbon and because of these girls, we had a wonderful time.

On the 11th day of April, our ship, the American ship, Siboney, was in port to take us to America. This would be a completely new experience for all of us. How exciting and sad too. Evening came and we were all on deck, watching the coast of Portugal disappear. Soon, seasickness hit us, except for dad and Jeannette. We stayed in our cabin and ate very little that first evening.

Next day we were sitting quietly on deck, watching people go by, talking cheerfully to each other. We heard several languages, but mostly French. This made us feel at home somewhat. After two days of sitting, Suzy and I had enough . We tried to forget our seasickness and joined the happy crowd. Soon we were part of a group of children, French-speaking, who walked together around the ship. Each time we passed a little stand, the store keepers would give us an apple or an orange.

It was particularly fun to watch the young adults play games they organized. We had a really great time, and the food was so good, we didn't t want it to end. Poor mom, she was sick the whole time and spent most of the crossing on deck on the lounge chair; sometimes even the nights.

On our way to America, on board the Siboney Ship.

8

NEW YORK/ELLIS ISLAND

Everybody was feeling the same excitement and expectations that evening. New York was close; the ocean was calmer. The dining room was full of life, double the amount of people than the previous days. After dinner, we rushed on deck hoping to get a glimpse of land, and stayed for a long time. Nothing! We went to bed, thinking only of tomorrow.

The first thing in the morning, after breakfast, we ran outside to join everybody who were just staring at the horizon. To add to our frustration, the sky became cloudy and a light fog developed. Discouraged, we returned indoors. By then, it was lunchtime. A very good distraction.

After lunch, we were back on deck. This time there was a commotion going on. People were looking with binoculars and seeing the promised land. As we were getting closer, the joy and excitement was indescribable.

Cries of admiration filled the air at the sight of the Statue of Liberty. To us, escaping the war, she was a true symbol of peace and prosperity. We couldn't tear ourselves away, and stayed on deck for hours, watching in awe the skyscrapers that spoke of power and money.

Dinner was announced, and the mood in the dining room was like a big party. Everybody was smiling and talking animatedly. After dinner, we went back on deck to contemplate the city illuminated; it was just like we had seen in pictures.

The next morning was not what we expected. Instead of visiting the city, and waiting for our ship to take us to our final destination, a group of us disembarked and got on a small boat that was to take us to Ellis Island. This small island is just at the entrance to the harbor. On it loomed a large building that looked like a fortress. Refugees who arrive and do not have the right documents are sent there to wait until they are processed. It could take days, and in the meantime you lived there like you were in a prison.

We were led to a very large room with big windows. There were quite a few people sitting around. We did the same, and waited. After a while, Suzy and I decided to walk over to the window, but this was not allowed and were told to go back to our seats. We could walk, just not stand by the window. So we did and bumped into a friend from the ship. To pass the time, we played cards together until the bell sounded for lunch.

They had us line up like prisoners, and each one of us was counted. Long tables were set up with benches on each side. The food was already served. Then back to the main room after being counted one by one. Except for one hour spent outdoors, we remained in that big room until dinner.

The same procedure was followed, with the counting of all the people, in and out of that room. When time came to sleep, women were separated from the men, even if they were married to each other. It was set up dormitory style. We were each given a towel and soap for our shower. The same grill door that closed behind us last night, opened again in the morning. Mom was sick of the whole thing. That day, we learned that there was a ship leaving for the Dominican Republic the following day. It was too bad mom was so impatient; with a little more time the Joint would have intervened and probably arranged for us to stay.

I certainly do not regret coming to Ciudad Trujillo in the Dominican Republic; life is simple here. For me, it was a wonderful place to grow up.

A gentleman escorted us to the Borinquen, another American ship. The mood on the Borinquen was totally different. These were people vacationing and they all spoke English. The waters were calmer, and the temperature warmer each day. We stopped in San Juan, where we didn't t waste any time to visit the department store, to be outfitted for the tropics, including hats and sunglasses. One more day at sea and we would arrive.

The first thing we saw were the palm trees. What kind of life was waiting for us? How civilized was this island, would we be the only white people there? As the ship was getting closer, the sirens sounded to announce its arrival. Now, every time I hear that sound, I think of that day, and all the emotions and confusion that went through each of us.

A gentleman from the Joint was waiting for us (we were not the only white people, after all). After going through Customs, he took us to a small hotel full of refugees. It was the 29th of April, 1941. We were starting a new life, in a new country, in a new world.

PART TWO -
WRITTEN 70 YEARS LATER

My story was meant to end here. It was buried in my things for 70 years. Then, at my grandson's wedding in Maryland, I met a French woman named Nicole who knew about me. She was very interested in my past; when and how I left Paris etc. I told her I had all the details on paper and would be glad to send it to her. Upon my return, I found my notebook, made copies and sent it to her as promised. Soon after, Nicole called me, all excited. She was moved by my story and by the fact it was written by a child. She felt it should be published and that is how it all started. It was written in French and I sat down to translate it. A few of my friends read it and they all had the same question: "What happened in the Dominican Republic?" And so, urged by my editor, Karen Bonnet, and my friends, I continued my tale below.

9

CIUDAD TRUJILLO - DOMINICAN REPUBLIC

The hotel hosted mostly German refugees. Father, fluent in five languages, was comfortable in his surroundings. After a few weeks, a house was found with three bedrooms and a front porch. It was in a residential area, close to the ocean.

Next, Suzy and I had to be registered for school. Mom had reservations to have us attend a public school. Somehow, she discovered a private school, not far from our house. The principal and owner was a charming woman, a mullato, who had studied in France. Mother pleaded her case: we left everything behind and had no money. She took us in, free of charge, delighted with the two cute French girls who didn't t know a word of Spanish.

Trujillo, dictator of the island since 1930, was feared by the Dominicans. We soon learned that it was best not to even utter his name in public. However, to us refugees, he opened his island and even donated a piece of land to the north called Sosua, to become a dairy factory. Many of the refugees went there to work, among them our father as an accountant. Sosua was a small village on the northern coast of Dominican Republic. It had nothing to offer, except beautiful beaches. At this particular time, Dominican Republic was the only country opened to refugees. Why my father chose to go to Sosua when he could have remained in the Capital, I don t know. My mother was not following him.

His decision to leave us, so soon after our arrival, with mom not knowing the language, was a step toward their separation and eventual divorce.

Trujillo also provided a building to be converted into a synagogue in the capital city. It was not long before we, (that is, mom) had a small group of friends. They were not French, but they spoke the language fluently. There was one couple, both Russians, no children; two single brothers from Poland, and a very kind single man from Rumania. We became very attached to this group; they were our family.

One day, our Rumanian friend said to mom, "You know, I want you to meet this couple, also Rumanian; they have a daughter the same age as Gisele." And so I met my new friend "Emilia." She spoke pretty good French, having lived in France for some time. We became inseparable.

Our resources were limited, there was no money for even small luxuries. Emilia lived at one end of El Conde (the one and only main street of Ciudad Trujillo) and me at the other end. We had no telephone to communicate, but it was understood between us that on days off from school, we would get together. One or both of us would start walking toward the other. Sometimes we met halfway, or Emilia would arrive at my house before I started out. Neither had even a few pennies for the bus. We made it work, and I don t remember ever having any misunderstanding.

There was little to do, due to lack of money, yet we were never bored. Trujillo had built a walk all along the ocean; we loved to go there and sit on a bench and talk and talk...and then there was the movies!

Father came to visit from time to time. He didn't t stay long. The atmosphere was always tense and unpleasant for us. We didn't t hear anything from France during those years. Later, we found out my aunt and uncle were hiding in the south of France, and my cousin, a few years younger than me, was sent to England with the Kinder Transport. Sadly, we learned in the late forties, when the war was over and we were able to communicate, that my grandmother was deported to Aushwitz, the death camp, and died on the train before it arrived. She was spared the worst of it.

A luxury hotel, facing the ocean, was being built. We often walked there to see its progress. When it was completed, mom was hired to work in its gift shop. Eventually, Suzy started to work as a secretary for a shipping company and later at this beautiful and new hotel called "Jaragua."

I loved life in the Dominican Republic. It suited my temperament. It was relaxed (mostly because of the heat) old fashioned, and romantic. For instance, men were very respectful of young girls, (good girls). The custom was a young girl did not go out at night without a chaperone. When she was dating, same story. Maybe that is the reason they didn't t have long engagements; they married very quickly. The island was also beautiful. It was very rocky where we were but I never tired of looking at those green palm trees with the blue ocean as a background. The beach was about three miles away. ccasionally we took the bus there, but never went swimming. It wasn't the proper thing to do in a public beach. We enjoyed the sand, the music and the food. Dominican women avoided the sun. They wanted to remain as pale as possible.

When I think back, I realize how warm and accepting the Dominicans were, so it was easy and natural to mix in when the occasion arose.

Probably around the age of 15, I would only listen to classical music on the radio, while Suzy liked the "Hit Parade," popular music of the time. She was pretty, loved to dance, and was invited to many parties. Of course, always with a chaperone. I was too young for those things yet. Music was everywhere; you heard it all the time. Dominicans loved to dance!

I was in charge of watching Jeannette while Mom worked. Suzy was too impatient with her. One day, Emilia and I were sitting by a small pool (not a swimming pool), and as usual, very busy talking as teenagers do, and didn't t realize Jeannette had fallen in the water until we heard her screams. To this day , Jeannette will not let me forget it.

The war was over now. Most of the refugees couldn't wait to emigrate to other countries as soon as possible. Mother had her plans too.

My parents divorced when I was 16 and father chose to return to Paris. Many years later, I learned why my mother was stuck with three children, and my father free as a bird. He was willing to take Suzy; she was almost an adult and was already working. My mother rather had me in mind. She wanted Suzy with her. It was a matter of survival, pure and simple, as she was looking ahead to our arrival in New York. I find it so strange that this was not discussed openly with us; after all, didn't we have anything at all to say about our future? We did as we were told; we were minors, and that was that!

Mother laid out her plan. I was going to quit school, and instead attend a commercial school where I would learn typing, stenography, and some accounting. This way, I would have a skill and could start working when we arrived in New York. It wasn't t what I wanted to be, but I never questioned it. I guess I knew deep down I would not win.

Fate had a surprise for me. I met my young man and first love where I studied. He was a refugee from Spain, came with his parents and two brothers and was quite a few years older than me. At first, he would walk me home only; then he would come and visit me, sometimes alone, other times with his brothers. From the beginning, mom gave me a hard time, and then actually forbade me to see him. Of course that didn't happen. She was working and couldn't keep track of where I was at all times.

Jose 's family was heading for Venezuela. Emilia's for Mexico, and we would soon be on our way to the U.S. I was so much in love by then, I seriously considered leaving with Jose. But I was really still a child, and didn't know how to go about it. Jose, being older, knew it wouldn't t work and so we both sadly accepted the inevitable.

As I said before, Suzy worked at the hotel Jaragua. One day, one of the guests, an American business man, needed a secretary to type some letters, and so Suzy was sent for the job. When it was completed, the gentleman offered her a tip. Suzy, inexperienced with the world, and not knowing what was proper, refused politely.

Back at home, she related the whole incident to us. Mom immediately said to her, if he should come back, tell him you don t want the money, but if he would give us an affidavit, that would mean the world to us. As refugees, we needed a sponsor to come to the U.S. and we didn't t know anyone living there. A few weeks later, the gentleman was back and asked for Suzy again. He happened to be of Jewish faith, and he was glad to do it when Suzy explained our problem.

Jose left, and then Emilia. I was filled with sadness. Too much was taken away from me all at once. Leaving Ciudad Trujillo, and going to another foreign country, where I didn't know the language was traumatic for a girl at 16, especially when my wish would have been to return to France.

Susie, Amelia, and Gisele

*Amelia (my friend) and Gisele in
the Dominican Republic.*

Gisele, at 14 years.

10
NEW YORK

The day came when we had all our papers too. We were flying for the first time to Miami first to thank our benefactor, and then to New York. We were pretty nervous about the flight itself. There was a stopover in Haiti. We were glad to get off the plane and feel solid ground under our feet. All four of us had been seasick. Mom said we would stay overnight in a hotel and continue the next day.

We met the kind gentleman who made all this possible. After a few days , it was on to New York. Our friends, the Russian couple, had arrived a few months before. Mom had asked them to find lodging for us. Unfortunately, the year was 1947, when a lot of G.I.'s were back from the war, getting married and settling down. It was impossible to get an apartment. The best they could do was a hotel room. We stayed there for a week. Mom was able to find a room in a rooming house, with two beds and a kitchenette in a closet, and no private bath. It didn't t come cheap either. The demand was great, so we had to live this way, four people in very small quarters, sleeping two in each bed until we found an apartment. It would take a year-and-a-half.

Mom was a fur finisher in Paris and she hoped to find a job in that line. It was April, the wrong season! She would have to wait until the fall. In the meantime, we had to eat. Suzy had a letter of recommendation from her last job and with that, she and I set out on the subway, downtown to Battery Place. We took the wrong train and ended up in Brooklyn.

We found the company, "Alcoa Aluminum," occupied several floors. Suzy was hired immediately as a secretary, and I, not knowing the language, was also hired to distribute the mail on all floors. I was happy to have a job and knew this job was not forever.

Mom too found herself a job in a coat factory. How she accomplished that without speaking the language, I don't know.

Shortly after our arrival in the rooming house, a German family moved in. They were refugees that had escaped to Bolivia, and like us, came to settle in the United States. They were three brothers; one with a wife and two children around Jeannette s age; one was single, and the other had a wife, no children. Their goal was to find a chicken farm and work together. After several trips to New Jersey and coming home empty handed, they made a decision to move to California.

I worked, ate and slept, but I had a hard time adjusting to the new life. Jose and I exchanged many letters, but as time went by, I knew it was useless and hurtful to keep hoping for the impossible, and I stopped writing.

I didn't t like New York. It felt cold and gray. I missed my sunny Caribbean island. I found the young girls in the office quite aggressive with the men, married or unmarried. I wasn't t used to see that. Also the waste in general, as young as I was, shocked me.

After we were somewhat settled, mom and I went to night school to improve our English. It was mainly conversation, which was good for me, because I had studied the grammar only in school. Suzy had worked for an American Company in Ciudad Trujillo, so she had picked up enough of the language to get by.

One day I received a letter from a young man who was attending the same class. I was going through a rough time that first year, trying to overcome all the different emotions that nobody seemed to notice, so I was not looking for an eligible bachelor. He wanted to take me out. He said he was sitting in the back of the classroom, and described himself. I had no idea who he was! So, the following week, we did connect and from then on started dating.

Leo was a German refugee, who had escaped the concentration camps in the south of France, along with his sister. Aided by the underground, they made their way to Switzerland where their grandparents lived. The Swiss government allowed them to stay on the condition they

would learn and work at only the trades dictated by them. And that is how Leo became a baker.

A lady friend of mom, from Ciudad Trujillo, was visiting us one day and proceeded to tell us about her first cousin who she had just met for the first time. He came from Egypt, where his brother and widowed mother still remained and were to follow later. She wanted Suzy to meet him. When they did, it was a mutual and immediate attraction.

A lot was happening all at once. Everybody was finding their niche. Our German friends found their farm in Sonoma, some 50 miles north of San Francisco. Gerhard, the single brother, took to writing to mom. He was a very kind and even handsome gentleman with a sense of humor. After settling down, the family invited mom to spend her vacation time with them, which we encouraged her to do. We certainly could handle everything, including Jeannette.

We had found an apartment in Brooklyn with two bedrooms. The whole block consisted of attached houses; old, but a great improvement from the rooming house. Mom worked late in season, so Suzy had taken over the cooking.

So it was all arranged, mom would go to California, for a much needed vacation.

When mom returned, Gerhard was writing to her regularly. And then came the marriage proposal. This presented a dilemma for mom. He wanted her there. There was no question about Suzy and me moving to California. Suzy was two years into the relationship and was not about to break up. As for myself, I was 19, and couldn't picture living with them, plus I was fond of Leo and hated the idea of another change in my life. In 1949, young girls stayed at home until they got married. It wouldn't t look good for Suzy and I to room together.

However, we wanted our mother to find happiness and were excited for her. The problem was solved this way: Suzy and Albert decided to get married and I would live with them in the same house we were living now. Jeannette was only 12 and had to be with mom. I was looking to get married, but we were not ready for that commitment. We needed more time to know each other. Also, we worried that Leo would be drafted in the Korean war.

It was, after all, a very bad arrangement as I was going to discover later. For one thing, Jeannette was separated from her sisters, and having to share her mother with this stranger, however nice he was. As for me, I had no friends or family to turn to, other than Suzy. Unfortunately for me, Suzy was completely engrossed in her new husband, and I was almost entirely ignored and on my own. I was totally miserable, and would break down and cry whenever I talked to mom. I couldn't help myself.

A year passed, and things didn't t get better at home. Leo did not get drafted. He was lonely too, living in one room in a couple's apartment.

We decided to get married. Mom came with my trousseau in a suitcase. The trip was too costly for Jeannette to come too. It was a very small wedding, with just the immediate family; about 10 people in all. The ceremony was at the Rabbi s house and later we celebrated in a well-known restaurant.

Emilia and I never stopped writing to each other. She married young and had three children. She and her husband went in the lumber business as her parents did. Leo and I visited her a few years after our marriage. It was like twins that were separated and just reunited. We could tell each other anything and everything without reservation.

Sadly, her husband died of a heart attack at age 39. By then, her lumber business was doing very well, so she was traveling a lot, coming to New York just to see a show and shopping. Of course, we saw each other every time. But, bad luck would not leave her alone. She married a second time. A few short years later, she would write me about her husband's strange behavior. One day, after disappearing for a few days, he called her from their place of business and asked her to come over. Thank God, she refused. The same evening, the police called her to say he had killed himself.

My friend did not live a long life. She had heart problems, and died at 59. Her daughter, knowing of our long friendship, found my address to give me the sad news.

Leo and I were blessed with two healthy daughters, and by now, three grandsons and three great granddaughters and counting—each one is wonderful in their own way. We had our share of economic failures, illnesses, lots of travelling, and happy events. We saw proudly our children become responsible and successful persons, and their children follow in their footsteps. We celebrated our 50th anniversary with friends and family 2 years before Leo s passing. Today, at 85, I am in reasonable good health, and grateful for the good things that came my way.

Gisele and Leo (my husband)
on our wedding day.

BIOGRAPHY - GISELE BAER

I was born in Paris, France, and lived there until I was eleven years-old. Even at that young age, I loved to tell stories to my sister which I made up as I went along, to be continued the next day, and so on.

My secret dream was to be a writer. Then, World War II broke out. It was June 1940 and everything changed. Now I had real stories to tell. How we left Paris, unknowingly, one day before the occupation. How we kept moving from town to town, always a step ahead of the Germans. Then the realization that we had to leave France, and it didn't matter where we went.

I was 15 years-old when I began writing in detail what happened to me and my family and how we were able to get out of France in turbulent times. This is my story——I hope you enjoy reading it.

www.ingramcontent.com/pod-product-compliance
Lightning Source LLC
Chambersburg PA
CBHW071802020426
42331CB00008B/2378